FINDING JESUS

A Walk with Him

FRANK BOAHENE

Published by
Hasmark Publishing
www.hasmarkpublishing.com

Copyright © 2021 Frank Boahene
First Edition

No part of this book may be reproduced or transmitted in any form or by any means, electronic or mechanical, including photocopying, recording or by any information storage and retrieval system, without written permission from the author, except for the inclusion of brief quotations in a review.

Disclaimer

This book is designed to provide information and motivation to our readers. It is sold with the understanding that the publisher is not engaged to render any type of psychological, legal, or any other kind of professional advice. The content of each article is the sole expression and opinion of its author, and not necessarily that of the publisher. No warranties or guarantees are expressed or implied by the publisher's choice to include any of the content in this volume. Neither the publisher nor the individual author(s) shall be liable for any physical, psychological, emotional, financial, or commercial damages, including, but not limited to, special, incidental, consequential or other damages. Our views and rights are the same: You are responsible for your own choices, actions, and results.

Permission should be addressed in writing to llinkc365@gmail.com

Editors: Kathryn Young
kathryn@hasmarkpublishing.com

Harshita Sharma
harshita@hasmarkpublishing.com

Cover Design: Anne Karklins
anne@hasmarkpublishing.com

Book Design: Amit Dey
amit@hasmarkpublishing.com

ISBN 13: 978-1-77482-104-6
ISBN 10: 1774821044

ACKNOWLEDGMENTS

All scriptures quoted in this book are from the New International Version (NIV) of the Bible.

DEDICATION

I would like to dedicate this book to my lovely wife, Mary Boahene, and to my beautiful children, the Boahene bunch. They light up my day, and through them, I am always able to see the goodness of God in every chapter of life. I love you all so much!

I would also like to dedicate this book to my leadership team at my church, Church 365. You guys are amazing! Your support and push over the years have made me so proud to be your leader. Your words of encouragement, prayers, and support have been my pillars, lending me support both physically and spiritually, and great foundation to the ministry that God has called me to serve. I love you all with the depths of my heart. I know that God will reward you for your great assistance and kindness.

CONTENTS

Introduction ix
Chapter 1: The Way to God 1
Chapter 2: The Importance of Finding Jesus 7
Chapter 3: Who is Jesus? 13
Chapter 4: The Genealogy of Jesus 20
Chapter 5: The Life of Jesus 25
Chapter 6: His Mission on Earth. 30
Chapter 7: Unstoppable Love 34
Chapter 8: Gateway of the Sheep 37
Chapter 9: Following Jesus 40
Chapter 10: Trial and Crucifixion 44
Chapter 11: The Compassion of Christ 48
Chapter 12: The Power of Christ. 51
Chapter 13: Jesus Unlimited 55
Chapter 14: Repentance 58
Chapter 15: Words of Jesus 61
Encouragement and Prayer of Salvation 66
About the Author 68
End Notes 69

INTRODUCTION

It is my hope that as you read this book, you will learn the importance of finding Jesus and knowing about his love for you. Some people who read this book may feel uncertain, thinking that Jesus' life and history are just part of a story. Yet, for me, belief in Jesus Christ is my conviction.

This book is my humble presentation to you. I am presenting Jesus to you. This is my most valuable and greatest joy. Whoever you are, I want you to know that Jesus loves you very much. He is the reason for your existence. He loved you before you existed, and he desires a relationship with you even today.

I put this book together so that you may have the opportunity to know who Jesus is, what he is about, and where he comes from. It is my prayer that as you read this book, you will come to know him, and he will reveal himself to you.

At the end of each chapter, I have placed a personal prayer for you to meditate on, if you wish. It is your choice to read the prayer aloud or silently. Then, take a few minutes to let the message resonate in your mind and heart.

Peace and blessings,
Frank Boahene

CHAPTER 1

THE WAY TO GOD

There is only one form of transit to God, and that is through Jesus Christ.

Finding Jesus is the Way

The way to God is extremely important because the path we take determines our destination. We cannot sit on the train of life and expect to make progress without having a sense of where we are going and how we should get there. Finding the true path to the ultimate destination gives our lives a sense of purpose, understanding, meaning, and fulfillment.

Finding this connection to God ensures that our lives are not empty and simply living day to day or paycheque to paycheque. Our connection to God gives us genuine purpose and a sense of meaning. We need to understand that not only is there a way to God, but we were created and formed with an intention and with a great plan. When we realize this, we are inspired to follow God's path.

In his book, *My Utmost for His Highest*, Oswald Chambers says it best: "Your priorities must be God first, God second, and God third, until your life is continually face to face with God."

If only God could become our utmost priority, we could dive deeper into intimacy with him. You may be asking yourself, how do I put God first? You put God first by *seeking after him*, *looking up to him*, and *trusting in him*.

However, we can only draw nearer to God through Jesus Christ of Nazareth. Jesus speaks the truth when he says, "I am the way, and the truth, and the life. No one comes to the Father except through me" (John 14:6).

Jesus is the connecting agent between the Father and us. There is no other medium between humanity and God. This is why it's necessary for every person to seek and find Jesus. Finding Jesus is the greatest landmark in the journey of one's life.

Many people believe that finding a spouse, an occupation, or even a new business venture is the prize-winning achievement in life. But how would you feel realizing that everything you have strived and worked for holds no eternal gain or value?

"What good will it be for someone to gain the whole world, yet forfeit their soul?" (Matthew 16:26).

Life is a journey in which we are all seeking something of great value. Whether we acknowledge it or not, we are all seeking. Often, the things we seek provide us with love, comfort, assurance, dependability, and protection, just to name a few.

Sometimes, the things we seek provide those values, but only on a temporary basis. We are then left empty, vulnerable, and looking to fill a specific void inside ourselves. There is nothing that can truly fill the gap in your heart except for Jesus Christ.

When God created us, he intricately wove a desire for love within our hearts. Every other kind of love you have or will experience is incomparable to the love of Jesus. If there is a primary suggestion that I could make to you concerning your journey in life, it would be to seek and find Jesus.

Heaven Sent

Our Father, God, has always reigned and ruled on his throne in heaven. Before the first coming of Christ, humanity remained engulfed in sin before a Holy God. Throughout the Old Testament, there was a constant need for God's people to offer sacrifices to atone for their sins. Leviticus 4:1–5:13 and 6:24–30 describe the specific priesthood offerings intended to make atonement for sin.

These Old Testament priests were given the responsibility to intercede on behalf of the lives of the Jewish people. Leviticus explains that the priests would carry the prayers of the people into the Holy of Holies, the most sacred inner sanctuary within the Tabernacle (temple) in Jerusalem. The priests would remain there praying for many days.

The Old Testament describes how the High Priest would go forth on the Day of Atonement (Leviticus 23:26–32) to the temple to make animal sacrifices on the day of spiritual cleansing of sin. The sacrifice on this holy day was required to atone for the sins of humanity as an offering to God.

This was how things were done before Jesus was released to come to Earth. God, being compassionate and all-loving, sent his only Son from heaven for the sake of you and me. In John 6:38, Jesus says, "For I have come down from heaven not to do my will, but to do the will of him who sent me."

Jesus came down out of obedience to the Heavenly Father. This is how you and I know that we are truly loved. Jesus, the Son of God, crowned in his glory and reigning as king, came down humbly in his majesty to redeem us for our sins.

Imagine that! Jesus came down from heaven as a sacrifice for all of us. God sent his only Son as a once-and-for-all offering to redeem all of humanity. Picture Jesus as a king, dwelling in his glory and majesty with thousands of angels. Yet, he decided to step out of the boundaries of his kingdom and everything he knew for the benefit of humanity.

Jesus walked away from glorious living to come down to Earth where he was disregarded, doubted, disgraced, and denounced by men. The very people he came to save denounced him, yet he humbled himself for their sake. For a king and ruler to humble himself in service for his people is almost impossible to imagine. Yet Jesus did this through his sacrifice and humility.

This is why Jesus is truly the way to God. God desired to make himself accessible to humanity on Earth. Therefore, Jesus came down from heaven to dwell among us and experience life on Earth just as we experience it. Jesus felt the pain, hunger, betrayal, struggles, difficulties, and hardships of human life. Christ's experience on Earth makes him more relatable to us. He experienced and overcame many challenges that we still experience today. His example shows us that we have the ability to triumph over any challenge that life throws our way because Jesus came before us and won the battle. Jesus came down from heaven to dwell among men so he could give us access to God through himself.

Truly, you and I are fully loved by an eternal and everlasting God.

Law to Grace

Before the first coming of Jesus Christ on Earth, God established his Law, which is described in the first five books of the Bible: Genesis, Exodus, Leviticus, Deuteronomy, and Numbers. These five books display the constitution of God's commands and portray God's decrees and instructions. The Law had a direct influence on the lives of the people of the era and is the basis of the Jewish holy scriptures, known as the Torah. These books were written prior to the first coming of Jesus and his fulfillment of the Law.

During this era of the Law, there was a need for sacrifice in the form of animals and burnt offerings. There was also a season and set time to put those offerings up before the Lord. In the era of the Law, compassion and grace were limited. This is evident throughout the Old Testament.

As you are reading this, I want you to imagine how life under the Law would be with the need for constant sacrifice to atone for sin. I think we can all agree that we would not want to live in such a time. But God had a great plan at hand. God decided to tear down the veil of separation between himself and humanity through the ultimate and one-time sacrifice of Jesus Christ. This was a precious sacrifice, a wonderful bridge, and a supernatural transition from *Law* to *Grace*. Thank God that you and I are no longer bound by the Old Testament laws, but through Jesus Christ, we have grace.

Jesus Christ offers humanity unmerited grace. This is a grace that we do not deserve, especially when we look at the state of our lives. In so many ways, we may have distanced ourselves from God, fallen short of his glory; yet still, he found it fit to extend his grace to humanity through his Son Jesus Christ. This is exactly what we need, though we may not always grasp the understanding that we truly need it. The grace of God says, *"I have a place for you in unity with me. I love you despite any of your faults and beyond your greatest imagination."*

Scripture assures us, "and all are justified freely by his grace through the redemption that came by Christ Jesus" (Romans 3:24).

PRAYER

Heavenly Father, I come to you in the only way that is possible through Jesus Christ, your Son. Draw me nearer to your presence. Help me to grasp the glory of your existence. In Jesus' name, amen.

CHAPTER 2

THE IMPORTANCE OF FINDING JESUS

Finding the missing piece to the puzzle makes it complete. Jesus is the missing piece in your life; find him, and you will see the full picture more clearly.

Why Finding Jesus Is Necessary

You may be asking yourself, "*Why is it necessary for me to find Jesus?*".

Whether we would like to admit it or not, we all are looking for something with great intent and profound depth to connect our lives to. Over our lifetime, we seek meaning and purpose for our existence. Some of us may seek this validation through work, living certain lifestyles, or from other people. But deep down, we are seeking comfort, assurance, a saviour to love us and uphold us. This saviour is Jesus. Jesus is truly everything that we seek. What is holding us back is that amongst all of our fruitless searching, we do not realize that we are really in pursuit of Jesus Christ.

So, the answer to your question is simple. *Finding Jesus is necessary for the security of your soul.* No one who has ever found Jesus and truly accepted him in their hearts has ever been the same afterward. One encounter with Jesus can change everything around you and within you.

John 4:1–42 speaks of a special encounter a woman had with Jesus at a well in Samaria. She was not just any woman but a woman who was deemed by society to be taboo. The scripture suggests that the woman may have been a prostitute living an immoral life.

Samaritans and Jews did not get along during Jesus' time. Charles Swindoll, in his book *New Testament Insights on John*, tells us that Jews despised Samaritans. To the Jews, Samaritans were no longer Jews but idolatrous because they intermarried with Gentiles and set up their own temple to rival the temple in Jerusalem. Jews even avoided passing through Samaria to avoid cultural "contamination." But on their journey back to Galilee, Jesus decided that he and his disciples would be taking the unusual route through Samaria.

A Samaritan woman would not have voluntarily associated with or spoken to a Jew she encountered. However, while the disciples were seeking food, Jesus broke through the woman's defenses that day at the well because he was always after the heart of a person. He did not care where the woman was from, or whether her culture was different, or whether she was living an immoral life at that moment. This observation provides an important lesson in the gospels and one that each of us must learn:

Jesus is not concerned with your background or your spiritual distance from him or the lifestyle in which you live. He is concerned only with capturing your heart.

In John 4:13–14, after asking the distrustful Samaritan woman for a drink of water, Jesus says to her, "Everyone who drinks of this water will be thirsty again, but whoever drinks the water I give them will never thirst. Indeed, the water I give him will become in him a spring of water welling up to eternal life."

Jesus got her attention. He offered her something she could not refuse. Jesus knew of her lack of trust, her desires, and her immoral lifestyle. He wanted to offer her something that would change her life forever.

Many of Jesus' fellow Jews would have disqualified the woman from God's grace because of her choice of lifestyle, but Jesus accepted her where she was. And so, Jesus desires to accept you—to receive you, transform you, and renew your life. When you are living in Christ, you will never thirst again, for he will satisfy your every need.

Jesus Revealed

Truthful intimacy is the only way we can truly know anyone. Even in our natural everyday relationships, before we can testify of knowing an individual, we must come to a level or place of intimacy. It is possible that you may know of Jesus in a traditional or religious manner, through Sunday preaching, your favourite online speaker, your reading, or simply what you have heard others say. However, nothing can ever replace an intimate relationship with Jesus.

So how do you get to this place of truly knowing him? Start by seeking to know Jesus on a greater and more personal level. Speak to him through prayer, study his words in New Testament for yourself, and most importantly, ask for a *revelation*.

Matthew 16:13–20 speaks of Simon Peter, a devoted servant of Jesus Christ. Jesus was Peter's mentor, teacher, leader, and more. One day, Jesus came to Philippi with Peter and the other disciples, and Jesus asked them, "Who do people say the Son of Man is?"

These disciples were those closest to Jesus. They prayed with him, dined with him, sat under his teaching and training, and even fellowshipped with him. Yet, they hesitated and struggled to answer his question. They finally replied, "Some say John the Baptist; others say Elijah; and still others, Jeremiah or one of the prophets." They were unsure and probably repeating what others had said.

I believe the disciples were hesitant and unsure because although they had been in proximity to Jesus for years, many of them had not received revelation or divine truth. Proximity does not on its own result in revelation and knowledge of the true nature of Christ Jesus.

Jesus asked again, "But what about you? Who do you say I am?"

Peter finally answered Jesus' question with understanding and revelation in verse 16. Peter said, "You are the Messiah, the Son of the living God."

Peter did not perceive who Jesus was by what people around him thought or said—whether they were Pharisees, religious leaders, the other disciples, or Jews they encountered in their travels; nor did Peter base it on his experience in walking with Jesus. Rather, Peter received supernatural revelation from God of Jesus' sovereignty and divine identity. Jesus confirms this by blessing Peter in verse 17 and saying, "for this was not revealed to you by flesh and blood, but by my Father in heaven."

Peter's revelation of Jesus Christ also enabled Peter to experience the presence of Jesus Christ in a way that the other disciples may not have known him. It is only once you receive a supernatural revelation of Jesus Christ that you can experience his power, glory, and presence. This supernatural revelation of Jesus is not simply uncovered by our logical minds, research into scripture, or life experience. It is based on supernatural revelation through the spirit of God. This is when your spirit and heart will begin to testify about the awesome existence of Jesus Christ.

The Pharisees and Scribes in Jesus' time were well-educated religious authorities within the Jewish culture who spent their time studying the law of the Torah. They studied the scripture so they would know who the coming Messiah would be. Unfortunately, when the Messiah came into their midst in the flesh, they rejected and denied him. Although the Pharisees and Scribes studied scripture about the coming Messiah, they did not appear to have a hunger and relentless desire to find him. It is only through true revelation and a great yearning for intimacy that Jesus can be revealed to an individual. Only when we hunger and thirst after his presence and desire intimacy with Jesus will he reveal his truth and personhood to us.

Our Heavenly Father is ready to reveal his Son to anyone *who has an open and ready heart to receive the master.* Will you open your heart and spirit to the knowledge of Jesus Christ?

Jesus in Your Life

Who do you know Jesus to be in your life? Do you truly know him, or do you simply know of him—based on what other people say? These are questions we should ask ourselves if we truly desire to come into greater fellowship with Christ Jesus.

Even after we find Jesus and accept him into our lives, we must strive to know him ever more deeply and intimately. Knowing Jesus on this intimate level ensures we are building our faith on a firm and established foundation based on his divine truth. Often, many profess to follow Jesus but simply have no understanding of who he truly is because they are not connected to a deep understanding of his words, his teachings.

The greatest blessing after finding Jesus is coming to the knowledge of his lordship by studying his ministry, his journey, and his life in the New Testament scripture, beginning with the gospels of Matthew, Mark, Luke, and John.

When you truly know Jesus, you can go into greater depth in your worship. Your purpose will be a spirit-filled Christian life. You will walk by faith—not by sight.

PRAYER

I pray for you, by God's divine grace, that you receive the revelation of Jesus by the power of the Holy Spirit. May the eyes of your heart, mind, and soul be open to this revelation. In Jesus' name, amen.

CHAPTER 3

WHO IS JESUS?

We can never get to God without knowing Jesus.

The Truth of His Identity

One of the most controversial questions that could ever be asked is *Who is Jesus?*

Differing opinions from both religious and nonreligious traditions try to explain who Jesus is, but there are few certainties about his history and identity.

Therefore, our knowledge of Jesus must not come merely from outward sources of historical or scholarly information, but it should come from personal revelation and understanding of God's word. In a secular world in which Jesus often is portrayed as a mere man, it can become difficult for many to truly grasp and perceive his identity.

Some traditions present Jesus as simply a prophet who was called to do God's work. Others speak of him as a servant, trailblazer, or teacher. Some even suggest Jesus never existed!

But Jesus is real. Matthew 1:23 declares at Jesus' birth that he will be called *Immanuel*, which means God is with us. This means Jesus is God in the flesh. This is a difficult doctrine for some to accept. This reluctance is mainly because people ask how a spiritual God can be a human?

In John 10:30, Jesus simply states: "I and the Father are one." This is what sets Jesus apart. Through his authority as God in the flesh, he can forgive our sins (Luke 5:20). All the prophets who came before Jesus in the Bible were only able to ask for mercy or intercede through prayer for the people, but only Jesus could personally forgive. The sins of man would be forgiven right then and there.

Jesus existed and reigned in his kingdom before the creation of this world. "In the beginning was the Word, and the Word was with God, and the Word was God" (John 1:1).

Jesus Christ in the Trinity

The Holy Trinity of God simply refers to one God made up of three persons. For many, this is a difficult concept to grasp. Each person in the Trinity has a specific role.

God the Father	God the Son	God the Holy Spirit
First Person of the Trinity (Head of the Trinity)	*Second Person of the Trinity* (God Incarnate—God Manifested in the Flesh on Earth)	*Third Person of the Trinity* (Spirit of the Living God) (God Manifested in Spirit)
Names: Yahweh, I am that I am, Jehovah, El Elyon, Jehovah Rapha	*Names:* Jesus Christ, Immanuel, Son of God, The Messiah, Anointed One	*Names:* Intercessor, Holy Spirit, Holy Ghost, Comforter, Spirit of Truth, Spirit of the Living God

Function: Creator, Ruler, Authority,	Function: Advocate, Redeemer of all life	Function: Revelator, Empowerer, Intercessor, Spiritual Conviction, Helper
Scriptures: Matthew 23:9, Revelation 1:8, Revelation 4:11, Isaiah 40:28	Scriptures: John 1:18, John 5:18, John 8:18, John 8:58, John 14:10, John 20:28	Scriptures: Genesis 1:1–2, John 14:15–26, Romans 8:14, 2 Corinthians 3:17, John 4:24

A clear understanding of the Holy Trinity is essential to understanding the identity of Jesus Christ. Not only is the Trinity fundamental to your personal knowledge and relationship with Christ, but also to the doctrine of Jesus.

The simplest explanation of the Trinity is in the natural form of an egg. Every egg has three layers: shell, egg white, and yolk. Although each part of the egg is individual, together, they make up the egg. This is a relative comparison to the Trinity. All persons of the Trinity are individual; however, they coexist to make up God as a whole.

In Genesis 1:26, God the Father says, "Let us make mankind in our image." Notice that the scripture does not say in *my* image but in *our* image. This shows that the three persons of the Trinity partnered in the creation of humanity. In Genesis 1:2, the Spirit of God (Holy Spirit) was hovering over the waters before any creative activity.

In John 10, Jesus stands before several challenging and doubting individuals. They cannot wrap their minds around his identity.

They ask, "How long will you keep us in suspense? If you are the Messiah, tell us plainly" (John 10:24).

Jesus finally answers the skeptics: "I and the Father are one" (John 10:30).

This concept of Jesus and God being one can be difficult for some people to understand. However, this important scripture enables us to understand and accept that Jesus is God. Jesus is God in the flesh. By declaring that *I and the Father are one*, Jesus affirms the doctrine that he is God manifested on Earth.

Matthew 25: 31–46 speaks about Jesus' authority to judge humanity and the nations. This solidifies his authority as God in the flesh because only God is able to make judgements over his creation and humanity. This is the reason that he is not to be seen as simply a prophet or historical figure. Jesus is to be worshipped and acknowledged as Lord over us all.

Jesus wanted his disciples to know that the Father they worshipped was in one union with him. This revelation confused the disciples at the time. We must not forget that although Jesus manifested in the flesh, he was not a natural man. Jesus was conceived and born of the Holy Spirit. He was born naturally but conceived supernaturally.

It is through Jesus that we have received the forgiveness of our sins. "In him we have redemption through his blood, the forgiveness of sins, in accordance with the riches of God's grace" (Ephesians 1:7).

Forgiveness is something that can only be manifested through God; therefore, the scripture affirms that Jesus is God.

The Mediator

Have you ever been in a position where you needed someone to defend you, someone to come to your aid or someone who could speak on your behalf? I am sure you have been in such a position; we have all been there or will be there someday.

Jesus is our personal defender and mediator. He is the mediator that every person needs in their life. Naturally, if you have ever been to court or had a legal issue, it is imperative that you have a lawyer or someone able to defend your case. Many cases allow you to represent yourself; however, the likelihood of success will lessen if you represent yourself. The reason we require legal aid is for defence, protection, and legal mediation to plead our case to both judge and jury. For that reason, most people seek legal representation when involved in a case. A professional lawyer or mediator has advanced knowledge because they have been trained, equipped, and studied to understand the case. In most circumstances, they have more leverage than the defendant.

What about your spiritual mediator? Who is standing in a place of authority to mediate on your behalf? You and I were born into sin, within no one to stand in the gap for our forgiveness. When Jesus came to die for us, we gained a great mediator. Jesus Christ is the mediator of our souls. He alone stood in the gap for us. "For there is one God and one mediator between God and mankind, the man Christ Jesus" (1 Timothy 2:5). Jesus is the mediator standing on our behalf between God and humanity. How great it is to know that we have been vindicated by the grace of Jesus!

Bread of Life

Matthew 5:6 says, "Blessed are those who hunger and thirst for righteousness, for they will be filled." This is one of the most popular biblical teachings of Jesus Christ and comes from what we call *The Sermon on the Mount*.

It was the desire of Jesus that the thousands of people listening to him would be filled, not simply with temporal satisfaction but everlasting satisfaction, and that they would never hunger again.

What is your hunger? What is your desire? By nature, we all hunger and desire after one thing or another, yet are we satisfied? It is possible to consume and eat yet never be satisfied fully.

Jesus Christ is means for satisfaction in our lives. Through him, we are fulfilled and never hungry. Jesus says, "I am the bread of life" (John 6:48). What exactly does that mean? Jesus was not speaking of physical bread—or quenching physical hunger; he was speaking spiritually. As much as we may search, there is nothing else that can satisfy the cravings of our souls. This is what many people miss.

Often, people live a full life materialistically and yet have an emptiness of their soul because they are not connected to God. In the same way that our physical body requires nourishment, so does our soul. The absence of food for your physical body is the absence of nourishment. Lack of food for your soul and spirit equals a missing link to eternity and life's purposeful fulfillment.

When we live a life without Jesus, we become spiritually malnourished, empty, and misguided. Without the *bread of life*, you may binge eat every other "food" that is offered to you: lust, greed, deception, self-satisfaction, and more. In the end, your soul will remain empty while longing for fulfillment.

The scripture tells us of one day when Jesus encountered 5,000 people who wanted to hear him (Matthew 14:13–21). After teaching the multitude and healing the sick, Jesus told his disciples to feed the people. A problem appeared as the disciples reported that they were short with physical provisions. They had only five loaves of bread and two fish. It seemed impossible to feed them. Jesus simply blessed and multiplied the food so that there was enough to satisfy everyone. There were even leftovers!

The revelation here is not just that Jesus multiplied the physical food, but rather that he fed the people with himself (the living word of God), making them full before they ate the physical food.

Dear friend, please know that Jesus is the only one who can satisfy your soul. Once you have received the bread of life, you will never hunger again.

PRAYER

Lord Jesus, I believe you alone can satisfy my every desire and hunger. May the Bread of Heaven feed me so that I am made whole. In Jesus' name, amen.

CHAPTER 4

THE GENEALOGY OF JESUS

In order to go forward with Jesus, we must trace back through the lineage of Christ. In this way, all the pieces of his existence are connected to us.

Although Jesus is God, he is also flesh. With that being said, since Jesus is flesh, his lineage and ancestry must be traceable. Think of it this way: Your bloodline and lineage have much to do with who you are and even sometimes the outcome of your life. This is the same with Jesus Christ. The tribe and blood lineage of Christ are very much connected to his assignment and the role that he would play on Earth during his initial coming.

From the Old Testament to the New Testament, there has always been a foretelling of Christ's coming through a specific bloodline and lineage. Understanding the genealogy of Christ helps us to anticipate the importance of his coming and later understand the role of his physical existence on Earth as recorded in the New Testament.

Jesus' Bloodline and Lineage

The Bible's Old Testament predicted that the Messiah would come from the line of David (Isaiah 9:6–7):

> "For to us a child is born, to us a son is given,
> and the government will be on his shoulders.
> And he will be called
> Wonderful Counselor, Mighty God,
> Everlasting Father, Prince of Peace.
> Of the greatness of his government and peace
> there will be no end.
> He will reign on David's throne
> and over his kingdom,
> establishing and upholding it
> with justice and righteousness
> from that time on and forever.
> The zeal of the LORD Almighty
> will accomplish this."

The gospels of Matthew and Luke, both list the genealogy of Jesus to confirm he was a descendant of David, thus making him a legitimate Messiah and claimant to Israel's throne. However, these two genealogies are somewhat different.

Possibly, they are different for complex Jewish cultural and legal reasons. Some scholars suggest that the genealogy in Matthew 1:1–17 refers to Jesus' *legal line* (Joseph is Jesus' legal adopted father under Jewish law) through David's son Solomon. These scholars further suggest that the genealogy in Luke 3:21–38 may refer to Jesus' *biological bloodline* through his mother Mary through David's son Nathan. Because women traditionally were not listed in direct descent in Jewish genealogies, Joseph may have been shown in Luke's version (instead of Mary) because he was the son-in-law of Mary's father (who had no other sons). But this is only an intriguing interpretation. Scholars have not been able to know with certainty why the two genealogies are different.

Comparison of Matthew's and Luke's genealogies

Matthew	Luke
	God, Adam, Seth, Enos, Cainam, Maleteel, Jared, Enoch, Mathusala, Lamech, Noah, Shem, Arphaxad, Cainanm Salam Heber, Phalec, Ragau, Saruch, Nachor, Thara.
Abraham, Isaac, Jacob, Judah, Perez, Hezron, Ram, Amminadab, Nahshon, Salmon, Boaz, Obed, Jesse, David,	Abraham, Isaac, Jacob, Judah, Phares, Esrom, Aram, Amminadab, Naasson, Salmon, Boaz, Obed, Jesse, David,
Solomon, Rehoboam, Abijah, Asa, Jehoshaphat, Jehoram, Uzziah, Jotham, Ahaz, Hezekiah, Manasseh, Amon, Josiah, Jeconiah,	Nathan, Mattatha, Menan, Melea, Ellakim, Jonam, Joseph, Judan, Simeon, Levi, Matthat, Jorim, Eliezer, Jose, Er, Elmondam, Cosam, Addi, Meichi, Neri,
Shealtier, Zerubbabei,	Salathiel, Zoraobabei
Abiud, Eliakim, Azor, Zadok, Achim, Eliud, Eleazar, Matthan, Jacob,	Rhesa, Joannan, Juda, Jeseph, Semel, Mattathias, Maath, Nagge, Eslim Naum, Amos, Mattathias, Joseph, Jannai, Meichi, Levim Matthat, Hell.
Joseph, Jesus	Joseph, Jesus

However, the important point is that these two genealogies reinforce Jesus' descent from David from one or both of his earthly parents, thus fulfilling the prophecy.

It is interesting to note that Matthew's genealogy is considered more complex than Luke's as it is organized into three sets of fourteen generations:

> "Thus there were fourteen generations in all from Abraham to David, fourteen from David to the exile to Babylon, and fourteen from the exile to the Messiah" (Matthew 1:17).

Each set has its own character. "The total of 42 generations is achieved only by omitting several names, so the choice of three sets of fourteen seems deliberate. Various explanations have been suggested: fourteen is twice <u>seven</u>, symbolizing perfection and covenant, and is also the *gematria* (numerical value) of the name <u>David</u>."[1]

Gematria refers to a code in which words in the Hebrew scripture are calculated according to the number value of the Hebrew letters. David's name in Hebrew is D (4) + W (6) + D (4) = 14.[2]

Why is Jesus' Lineage Important?

Why is the lineage of Christ important? Think about why your own family's history may be important to understand your own identity.

In Luke, Jesus' lineage traces all the way back to Adam, the first man in creation. Adam, as we know, first opened the door for sin, which has affected humanity throughout our history.

Several of the mothers mentioned in Matthew's account were well-known sinners as well. Rahab was a prostitute, Bathsheba committed adultery with David, Tamar posed as a prostitute to seduce Judah.[3]

Why did Matthew include these colorful and notorious women and not the more respectable Jewish matriarchs in Jesus' lineage? Perhaps Matthew wanted to emphasize that even Jesus' earthly bloodline was no different than our own. The existence of sin, in general, is why there was the need for Jesus, the redeemer, the one who would wash away our sins.

Abraham, whom God called to be the founder of a new nation, was an important part of Jesus' genealogy. God promised that he would bless Abraham's lineage and the generations to come. This promise would be fulfilled through Jesus Christ.

It is important that we identify and understand the lineage and the many generations that led to Jesus Christ because knowing what came before Christ enables us to know the future of who he was destined to become. Looking into the lineage may seem like a dry history lesson, but truly what it does is give us further clarity into the reason for the coming of Jesus. Jesus Christ was the fulfillment of his bloodline. Everything leads to Jesus.

PRAYER

Precious Jesus, you are the one who was, is, and is to come. May I know you even more. In Jesus' name, amen.

CHAPTER 5

THE LIFE OF JESUS

The precious life of Jesus should be understood in order for us to have intimacy with him. We must know how and where he prayed, when he broke bread, and when he had trials and tribulations. All these things bring us closer to him!

God in the Flesh

Even with the fullness of his authority, Jesus was subject to human life like you and me. "The Word became flesh and made his dwelling among us" (John 1:14).

Although he was God in the flesh, he submitted himself in humility, living life on Earth as a normal being. Not only was he born and lived as a normal human being, but he remained sinless throughout temptations and trials. By living thus, he was made perfect.

"For it was fitting for us to have such a high priest, holy, innocent, undefiled, separated from sinners and exalted above the heavens" (Hebrews 7:26).

It would be easy to believe that as a king in heaven, Jesus should have led an easy life while on Earth, but his life was quite the opposite. His early years were challenging.

Seven Major Turning Points

Jesus experienced seven major turning points in his life: birth, baptism, public ministry, transfiguration, crucifixion, resurrection, and ascension.[4]

Birth

The birth (nativity) of Jesus is described in two of the gospels: Matthew and Luke. These two gospels are clear on several assertions:

- Jesus was not the natural son of Joseph (the betrothed of Mary).
- Jesus was miraculously conceived in Mary's womb by the Holy Spirit.
- Jesus was born in Bethlehem with angels proclaiming him saviour to the world.
- Jesus was descended from Abraham through the line of David, thus fulfilling the Old Testament prophecy of the Messiah.

Baptism

Jesus' baptism by John the Baptist marked the beginning of Jesus' public ministry. Matthew, Mark, and Luke state that John was reluctant to baptize Jesus because he recognized that Jesus was sinless. "I need to be baptized by you, and do you come to me?" (Matthew 3:14)

After his baptism, the Holy Spirit descended upon Jesus, and a voice from heaven proclaimed, "You are my beloved Son, in whom I am well pleased" (Mark 1:9–11).

Following his baptism, Jesus traveled alone to the Judean desert to fast for forty days and nights. During this time, Satan tried to tempt Jesus, but Jesus forthrightly rebuffed him. It is said that Jesus set the standard for us when it comes to resisting temptation: stand your ground in the face of temptation and rely on God's word (Matthew 4:1–11).

When Jesus demanded, "Away from me, Satan," the devil instantly departed, and angels came to attend Jesus and brought nourishment. Jesus then returned to Galilee to begin his ministry.

Public Ministry

The gospels tell us that Jesus' ministry began when he was thirty years of age following his baptism. Jesus began in the general region of Galilee and gathered twelve disciples (apostles) to accompany him on his ministry. Jesus began teaching his disciples, preaching to growing crowds from Galilee to Judea, and performing miracles. John speaks of several miracles in his gospel but also tells us that Jesus performed many more miracles than those listed (John 20:30).

Jesus' miracles ranged from turning water into wine and healing the sick to raising his friend Lazarus from the dead. During his ministry, Jesus' identity as the Christ (Jewish Messiah) and Son of God is gradually revealed to his disciples.

Transfiguration

The transfiguration is considered one of the miracles of Jesus and is described in the gospels of Matthew, Mark, and Luke. This miracle is considered unique in that this miracle happens to Jesus himself. Jesus took Peter, James, and John with him to a mountain to pray. While praying, Jesus was transfigured before their eyes. "His face shone like the sun, and his clothes became as white as the light. Just then there appeared before them Moses and Elijah, talking with Jesus" (Matthew 17:2–3). Jesus tells the disciples not to tell anyone what they had seen.

Crucifixion

All four gospels describe Jesus' arrest, trial, and crucifixion in great detail.[5] Because his teachings and miracles threatened the power of the Jewish priests and the Sanhedrin (Jewish judicial body), the authorities sought to arrest Jesus when he came to Jerusalem. Jesus was betrayed by his disciple Judas Iscariot, arrested, condemned to death, and ordered to be crucified by Pontius Pilate, the Roman Governor. Jesus knew and accepted his role in God's plan. His death was a willing sacrifice for humanity. Jesus' crucifixion was a critical event because of the doctrines of salvation (saving humanity from sin, death, and separation from God) and atonement (the forgiving of sin through death and resurrection of Jesus).[6]

Resurrection

The death and resurrection of Jesus is the foundation of Christianity.[7] Jesus knew his destiny and prophesied his death and resurrection to his disciples.

"Now Jesus was going up to Jerusalem. On the way, he took the Twelve aside and said to them, 'We are going up to Jerusalem, and the Son of Man will be delivered over to the chief priests and the teachers of the law. They will condemn him to death and will hand him over to the Gentiles to be mocked and flogged and crucified. On the third day he will be raised to life!'" (Matthew 20:17–19).

After his resurrection, Jesus was seen by many of his followers and spoke to several of them. The meaning of Jesus' resurrection is a promise that all believers in Christ will be resurrected from death.

One of the key factors of Jesus' resurrection is not only that he rose again to life but that he overcame the power of death. The Bible explains to us that the wages of sin is death (Romans 6:23). Ultimately, if Christ could not overcome death, then he would also not be able to overcome sin because sin equals death.

Christ's resurrection reassures anyone who believes in his victory over sin and death. His resurrection enables us to know that we are not bound by sin, but rather we are liberated by his resurrection power.

Romans 6:23 concludes with this promise: "…the gift of God is eternal life in Christ Jesus our Lord."

Ascension

The Ascension refers to Jesus Christ physically leaving Earth and rising into heaven. According to the gospels, Jesus ascended forty days after the resurrection in the presence of eleven of his disciples. Before he ascended, he told them, "All authority in heaven and on Earth has been given to me. Therefore, go and make disciples of all nations, baptizing them in the name of the Father and of the Son and of the Holy Spirit, and teaching them to obey everything I have commanded you. And surely, I am with you always, to the very end of the age" (Matthew 28:18–20).

PRAYER

Lord Jesus, as I have learnt about your life, let it be my standard and my guide. Help me to follow your pattern of lifestyle. In Jesus' name, amen.

CHAPTER 6

HIS MISSION ON EARTH

The greatest mission that must be known to humanity is the assignment that Christ took up for you and me. Knowing fully the end result, he humbled himself for our sake.

What Jesus Came to Do

Jesus Christ had a mission. He was sent with a purpose that was to be fulfilled on Earth. He was not sent simply to mingle with humans or to experience human life. He had an assignment from God, and that assignment involved all of humanity. God had a vision to permanently redeem humanity from sin and destruction, and Jesus was assigned to perform this redemption. We are so fortunate to be a part of God's divine plan.

He Was Born with Purpose

As all of us are born into this world, so was Jesus. There were many obstacles to the first coming of Christ.

First, Jesus was not naturally conceived by man but supernaturally by God, through the power of the Holy Spirit. The scripture tells us that his mother Mary, a young virgin, was betrothed to a man named Joseph when an angel told her that she was to conceive a special child by the Holy Spirit.

"The Holy Spirit will come on you, and the power of the Most High will overshadow you. So the holy one to be born will be called the Son of God" (Luke 1:35).

What a remarkable birth this was to be and an amazing testimony to God's grace.

Another obstacle was that Joseph initially doubted Mary's supernatural explanation for her pregnancy. He knew that Mary was a noble and decent woman, but because of the unexpected pregnancy right before their wedding, he no longer wanted to continue the betrothal and planned to divorce Mary quietly.

But God had specifically chosen Joseph to be Jesus' earthly father and so sent an angel in a dream to console Joseph and encourage him to support Mary.

"An angel of the Lord appeared to him in a dream and said, 'Joseph Son of David, do not be afraid to take Mary home as your wife, because what is conceived in her is from the Holy Spirit. She will give birth to a son, and you are to give him the name Jesus, because he will save his people from their sins'" (Matthew 1:20–21).

Other obstacles included persecution from authorities here on Earth. After Jesus was born, Magi from the east came to Jerusalem and inquired of King Herod about the birth of a special child. "Where is the one who has been born king of the Jews? We saw his star when it rose and have come to worship him" (Matthew 2:2).

Herod was disturbed by this threat of a Messiah and feared that his kingdom would be shaken and overturned. He ordered all boys under two years of age to be killed. What Herod failed to understand is that Jesus did not come to reign over any earthly kingdom. The dominion, sovereignty, and kingdom of Jesus were established in heaven far before the creation of the Earth.

During this dangerous time, an angel from God warned Joseph of Herod's plans and told him to take his family and escape to Egypt. Joseph and his family did not return to Israel until after Herod's death years later.

Every obstacle to Jesus' birth and survival was swept away by God's divine intervention. Jesus was born with a purpose, and nothing was going to stop him from completing God's plan.

Jesus Came For You

John 3:16 says, "For God so loved the world that he gave his one and only begotten Son, that whoever believes in him shall not perish but have eternal life."

This is the gospel in a nutshell. Jesus came to us out of obedience to the will of the Father, and God, being so loving, wanted us to have everlasting life. Imagine that!

It is amazing that the Lord would think so highly of you and me to offer us everlasting life with him. This essentially means you and I can be saved from the destruction of this world. One day, the world and everything within it will perish, and all things will come to an end. But the scriptures say that whosoever believes in Jesus shall have eternal life.

Did you know that there is a second life after this life you are presently living? The second life is what you and I will face in eternity. If we receive Jesus and believe in him, then we are guaranteed everlasting life. This means we will never die but will reign and fellowship with him after our natural life comes to an end.

Jesus came for no other reason than this. What man deemed as impossible, God made possible through his Son (Luke 18:27).

Never was the mission of Christ on Earth an easy one. He was born despite obstacles facing his coming. He was threatened, disgraced, rejected, and doubted by his own people, but he remained faithful to God's task because of his love for you and me.

PRAYER

Lord Jesus, I am so grateful that you came to redeem my life and the lives of so many souls. Do not allow us to forget your great sacrifice. In Jesus' name, amen.

CHAPTER 7

UNSTOPPABLE LOVE

True love cannot be seized, quenched, or resisted even in the midst of turmoil.

Love That Cannot Be Measured

Jesus' love is like nothing you have ever experienced—it's a love that cannot be measured or described simply. John 15:13 says, "Greater love has no one than this: to lay down one's life for one's friends."

Who else would lay their life down on your behalf? Jesus is not only a friend but a friend that you have never met. Before you came into this world, Christ already loved you and loves you still. I know that may seem difficult for you to comprehend, but it is true.

1 Corinthians 13:4–8 describes Christ's love for us through his dedication and commitment to ensuring that we are saved:

"Love is patient, love is kind. It does not envy, it does not boast, it is not proud. It does not dishonor others, it is not self-seeking, it is not easily angered, it keeps no record of wrongs. Love does not delight in evil but rejoices with the truth. It always protects, always trusts, always hopes, always perseveres. Love never fails."

His is a love that had no ends or barriers. It is unstoppable.

Nothing Could Stop Him

When you are truly loved or cherished by someone, they will go to great lengths to ensure their love is made known. Jesus Christ experienced societal, religious, traditional, governmental, demonic, and spiritual barriers all because of his love for people. He did not allow what the Pharisees, Sadducees, religious leaders, or governmental leaders said to stop him from manifesting his love for humanity. Not even Satan, the father of lies, could stop him. Jesus was tempted, tormented, tortured, and everything in between. Yet, he still held onto the promise of his love.

You and I are called the "bride" of Christ according to scripture in Revelation 19:7. Jesus is the bridegroom, and we are the bride. Our relationship with Jesus is not a romantic one, but it is 'agape' love. This Greek word refers to the fatherly love of God for humans, as well as our reciprocal love for God.[8]

In the same way a husband is bound and committed to his wife, this is how Christ has bound himself to us through grace. We are his beloved, and he is the lover of our soul.

He Loves You Unconditionally

Jesus loves you as you are, despite your lifestyle, despite what you have done today or will do tomorrow.

"For I am convinced that neither death nor life, neither angels nor demons, neither the present nor the future, nor any powers, neither height nor depth, nor anything else in all creation will be able to separate us from the love of God that is in Christ Jesus, our Lord" (Romans 8:38–39).

PRAYER

Dear Lord, despite everything, I am glad your love is available to me. Give me insight and help me to understand that your love is enough for me. In Jesus' name, amen.

CHAPTER 8

GATEWAY OF THE SHEEP

The safest path sheep can take is the path the shepherd leads them on.

Jesus is a Shepherd

Sheep, by nature, are docile creatures who often lose their way. They are known for roaming, wandering, and often losing the direction of their pathway. There is one individual, however, who keeps count of the sheep and ensures that they are all in check and accounted for. That individual is the shepherd.

A shepherd holds the responsibility, accountability, and care for the sheep. When sheep lose their way, the shepherd is anxious and concerned. Remember that Jesus says it is right for the shepherd to leave the ninety-nine sheep safely in the flock to go and find the one lost sheep (Luke 15:4). He understands the value and importance of every individual sheep.

Would you agree that being a shepherd is not easy? How is it possible for one shepherd to guide so many sheep? No matter how tired the shepherd is, he never gets tired of guarding the sheep. He never tires of going after the lost sheep.

It is easy for us to get sidetracked in life. Sometimes we lose our path, and sometimes we fall out of line. These are all expected instances within the journey of life. What do you do when you feel as though you've lost your path? Who do you turn to? Where do you go?

In Christianity, Jesus is our great shepherd. He is consistently guarding and pursuing as we are his wandering and sometimes lost sheep. Though we are many, each one of us is loved, cared for, and protected under the watch of Christ. Jesus can be the shepherd of your life if you allow him. He will take care of you and keep you on the right path. Just in case you ever feel lost, you can also come back to the shepherd. He is ever ready to receive you!

Remember that the greatest predators of sheep are coyotes and wolves. These predators pursue lost sheep to devour them. In the very same way, the scripture tells us that Jesus says, "The thief comes only to steal and kill and destroy; I have come that they may have life, and have it to the full" (John 10:10). While the enemy is seeking to devour the sheep, Jesus, the Good Shepherd, is guarding his flock, keeping them safe and within sight.

Jesus is a Gateway

Not only is Jesus a guardian, but he is a gateway for the sheep. What is a gateway? A gateway is a path that regulates entry and exit. The one who controls the gateway is crucial because he will determine what goes in and what comes out. Therefore, it is through Christ that the sheep can safely enter the barn. Without the gatekeeper, the sheep will not have a haven in which to dwell.

"Therefore Jesus said again, very truly I tell you, I am the gate for the sheep" (John 10:7).

As we connect ourselves to Jesus, and he becomes our Lord and saviour, we automatically gain a personal gatekeeper.

Not only does Jesus declare himself as the gateway, but he promises salvation to any of the sheep that will enter.

"I am the gate; whoever enters through me will be saved. They will come in and go out, and find pasture" (John 10:9).

Jesus has given us divine access to enter the gate of salvation through his divine grace. What a great privilege you and I have to be a follower of a great shepherd. Each person's life has a gateway. When Jesus is not in our lives, we are prone to have an unguarded gateway. People come in and out. Opportunities and circumstances enter and exit. Joy, sadness, trials, and tribulations enter because this is the reality of life.

What circumstances or people have gained access through your gateway into your life? Whatever it may be, when you find and connect yourself to Jesus, he will ensure that whatever enters the gate will not harm his sheep. No one else can do this for you. If you have found Jesus, you have found a good shepherd.

When we become his followers, Jesus guides and comforts us through our trials.

PRAYER

Oh Lord, you are the Great Shepherd, the instructor of all my ways. Please keep me on the path of eternity and intimacy with you. In Jesus' name, amen.

CHAPTER 9

FOLLOWING JESUS

After we find Jesus, we must follow him.

Follow His Lead

Jesus Christ is our great head and leader. He is the one who leads our path into peace, abundance, salvation, and eventually, eternity. A key factor in having a personal relationship with Jesus is not simply *finding* him but *following* him.

It is one thing to find someone, and it is entirely another thing to follow. Following means that there is a great level of commitment and unity to the journey. Not everyone in the scripture found and followed Jesus. In fact, most of the encounters that took place in the scripture were those who found Jesus but were too afraid or reluctant to follow him.

For instance, the rich man described in Matthew 19:16–30 was reluctant to follow Jesus. This rich man located Jesus during his ministry but could not seem to commit to following him. Why? When we carry on in Matthew's story, we come to find that it was because he did not want to sacrifice his wealth. Therefore, he forfeited the call to follow Jesus.

Following Jesus means we must sacrifice and walk where he is leading. Jesus himself led a life of purpose and sacrifice. Therefore, anyone who decides to follow him would also walk such a path. When we declare Jesus as our Lord and personal saviour, we must be committed to following him, not simply for a moment, not as part of a phase, but for a lifetime. As we follow him, we stay close to him so that we can walk in his footsteps.

Jesus' Promise

Have you ever felt that you are constantly walking in darkness with no hope? The world can be a very dark place of confusion, manipulation, and depression. What would following Jesus mean in a world like this?

Jesus made a special promise when he said, "I am the light of the world. Whoever follows me will never walk in darkness, but will have the light of life" (John 8:12).

Following Jesus connects with this promise. Though there are many sacrifices that come with following his lead, there are also many promises to be manifested. Jesus promises us that we will be rewarded for following him in this life and in eternity. This is his special promise to us. Jesus offers us a great level of assurance as his followers. We are given intimacy, peace, joy, hope, light, guidance, grace, salvation, and new life. When you and I make up our minds to follow Jesus, we become recipients of these benefits and more.

Following Jesus is a very personal decision and may come with challenges. However, a commitment to do so is also paired with the promise of a blessed life following the Light of the World, confident of eternal life.

In the Midst of Chaos

Amid all the chaos in this world, following Jesus gives us assurance, safety, and direction while we navigate through life's problems and choices. Jesus promises us his guidance and encouragement as we walk the path where he leads us. He promises us his faithfulness if we choose to follow him.

Following Jesus enables you to walk a path in a life of purpose. He is a perfect guide to follow because he exemplifies love, humility, kindness, compassion, and a fulfilled life according to God's purpose for us.

Ultimately, following Jesus means journeying from pain and chaos to a destination of peace, salvation, and eternal life.

Practical Ways of Following Jesus

There are many practical ways of following Jesus:

- Read your Bible every day.
- Pray daily for guidance, strength, and inspiration.
- Talk to Jesus through the connection of the Holy Spirit.
- Fellowship with other Christians.
- Practice fasting to draw closer to the spirit of Christ.
- Find a Bible study group or church home (the body of Christ).
- Live the Word of God in your thoughts, words, and deeds.
- Practice the characteristics of Jesus Christ in your daily life.

As you grow in understanding of Jesus' life and teachings, you will be drawn to other ways to strengthen your discipleship.

Above all, practice what Jesus answered when asked by his disciples about the most important commandments:

The most important is "Hear, O Israel: The Lord our God, the Lord is one. Love the Lord your God with all your heart and with all your soul and with all your mind and with all your strength. The second is this: 'Love your neighbor as yourself.' There is no other commandment greater than these" (Mark 12:29–31).

PRAYER

Lord Jesus, I want to follow your lead. Yours is the path of peace and life. Guide me in all my ways. In Jesus' name, amen.

CHAPTER 10

TRIAL AND CRUCIFIXION

His death brought us life, his suffering brought healing, and his captivity brought us liberty.

What Was the Purpose of Jesus' Crucifixion?

As we have discussed, Jesus' crucifixion was one of the major turning points in his earthly life. But, what was the purpose of his death on the cross?

First of all, Jesus' trial and crucifixion display his committed obedience to God's plan. He knew from the beginning of his ministry what his fate would be. He tried to inform his disciples of his mission, but they had a hard time understanding what he was trying to tell them.

"He said to them, 'The Son of Man is going to be delivered into the hands of men. They will kill him, and after three days he will rise.' But they did not understand what he meant and were afraid to ask him about it" (Mark 9:31–32).

Despite his sorrow at his impending death, Jesus accepted his fate and showed his obedience to God in the Garden of Gethsemane. "My Father, if it is not possible for this cup to be taken away unless I drink it, may your will be done" (Matthew 26:42).

Secondly, Jesus understood his role in God's plan with his death a willing sacrifice for humanity's salvation. Before Jesus came, the animal sacrifices by the priests had to be performed daily because the priests knew they were not capable of forgiving sin. They knew only God could forgive sin. That was a major reason Jesus was condemned by the priests. They accused Jesus of blasphemy because he told people they were forgiven for their sins.

Although Jesus was accused, tried, and condemned, he was innocent of committing any crime. He was not a murderer, adulterer, nor did he commit any sin against his society or culture. He was only telling the truth in his teachings.

Like the innocent lambs the priests sacrificed, Jesus lived in this world sinless, innocent, and without blame. Jesus understood that his death would be a "once and for all" sacrifice that would save humanity forever from sin, death, and separation from God. Animal sacrifice would no longer be necessary for the reconciliation of God and humankind. Forevermore, atonement would come through the sacrifice of Jesus Christ on the cross. Jesus died to ensure all men have the opportunity to be free from the bondage of sin and worldly temptations.

Thirdly, there is no more powerful image of redemption than Jesus forgiving the penitent thief on the cross beside him. We don't know the thief's history or crime, but he rebukes the other thief's insults, willingly confesses his own guilt, proclaims Jesus' innocence, and asks Jesus to remember him in heaven. Jesus replies to him as the thief becomes the first sinner to be redeemed by Jesus' sacrifice. "Truly I tell you, today you will be with me in paradise" (Luke 23:43).

Just as Jesus saw into the thief's heart and heard his penitent words, Jesus knows our hearts and offers us forgiveness and redemption and the chance to be in heaven with him.

Jesus' resurrection fulfills his promise. Just as Jesus defeated death and rose from the grave, so too will those of us who find Jesus and willingly follow him.

Crucified in Body and Spirit

There is no doubt that crucifixion was intended to be a gruesome punishment for those who challenged the power of Rome. The sentence was reserved for slaves, criminals, and enemies of the Roman Empire. It was a humiliating and terribly painful way to die for those so condemned.

But the crucifixion of Jesus Christ was different from those of other men because Jesus was not only crucified in his flesh but also in his spirit. Jesus submitted to the torture and cruelty of crucifixion so that his body could die and then be resurrected in a symbolic victory over death. His spirit, however, could never die.

"Father, into your hands I commit my spirit" were Jesus' last words on the cross before he died (Luke 23:46).

The crucifixion symbolizes for those who follow Jesus that while our bodies will die someday, our spirits are eternal simply because of Jesus.

Jesus testifies this truth in John 11:25–26. "I am the resurrection and the life. The one who believes in me will live, even though they die; and whoever lives by believing in me will never die."

It is important to take time to reflect on the crucifixion of Jesus, not simply once a year on Good Friday, but every single day. Reflecting on the death of Jesus brings us a greater perspective of his love and sacrifice.

PRAYER

Heavenly Father, I thank you for the sacrifice of your Son Jesus. I know that through his surrender, I am made whole, I am healed, I am delivered, and I am blessed. In Jesus' name, amen.

CHAPTER 11

THE COMPASSION OF CHRIST

His mercy and grace are matchless. Great is his faithfulness to us.

Compassion and Mercy

As shown during his ministry, Jesus Christ was a man of compassion. His compassion was even for those who hated him the most. Often when Jesus came in contact with a large crowd, he showed compassion for their physical distress and hunger. The miracles of healing Jesus performed were manifested through his power because of his compassion and mercy.

Once, when Jesus and his disciples were leaving Jericho, they were approached by two blind men who cried for mercy. Jesus stopped and addressed the men.

"'What do you want me to do for you?' he asked. 'Lord,' they answered, 'we want our sight.' Jesus had compassion on them and touched their eyes. Immediately they received their sight and followed him" (Matthew 20:32–34).

Jesus also showed his compassion and mercy by forgiving people of their sins. His compassion was demonstrated by his kindness, sympathy, generosity, and forgiveness. By following Jesus, we can emulate his compassion by showing these same attributes to others. Forgiveness of sin, however, is something only Jesus has the power and authority to do.

Throughout his time on Earth, Jesus showed that he was passionate about humanity. He loved people, which is why he desired that all people might be healed, delivered, and saved through him. Whenever Jesus would go into towns, villages, and cities to preach, people swarmed to his side. They gathered not only to hear his powerful teachings but also to draw from his great compassion.

Jesus healed and touched many lives not only because he was the son of God but because he had compassion for the soul of mankind. Living on the Earth gave him the opportunity to see and feel the pain humanity faced from birth to death. This is the reason that hope in Jesus is not restricted to class, culture, tradition, gender, society or even the rules and regulations of man.

Jesus saw each soul, and his heart reached out to those who were in dire need of his loving touch. He loved the poor, the leper, the widow, the blind, and even his enemies.

For us today, the compassion of Jesus Christ is poured out by his love for all of humanity.

Love for Humanity

Jesus is loving, kind, and empathetic toward all people. He is moved with love for those who are disabled, sick, or ostracised by society. He has love and compassion for those who are lost, lonely, and rejected.

During his ministry, Jesus dined with, conversed with, and healed those who many believed he should have nothing to do with, such as lepers, prostitutes, tax collectors, and sinners.

Jesus sees the brokenness and loneliness of humanity. Jesus is aware of the scars, turmoil, and troubles that come during the journey of life. Having experienced life as a man on Earth, Jesus is even more empathetic and loving toward humankind. He knows us, he understands us, and he loves us.

It was Jesus' love for humanity that led him to be God's sacrificial lamb.

PRAYER

What a great saviour you are. You see what man cannot see. You feel the cry of the broken-hearted. Thank you for your endless compassion towards me. I love you Jesus. In Jesus' name, amen.

CHAPTER 12

THE POWER OF CHRIST

By his power, we are raised up. In his power, we are triumphant. Through his power, we touch lives.

Where Does Jesus' Power Come From?

Jesus Christ has been given all power and authority to reign over humanity by God. Jesus told his disciples that he had been given authority to operate in heaven and on Earth (Matthew 28:18). Peter said all of the angels, authorities, and powers have been made subject to Jesus in heaven (1 Peter 3:22).

God the Father gave Jesus the authority and dominion over everything on Earth. The well-known Bible passage says that every knee shall bow, and every tongue shall confess that he is Lord (Philippians 2:10–11).

How Does His Power Manifest?

The power of Jesus is manifested throughs the workings of his hand. Jesus' power was evident in his actions and manifestations while on Earth. He consistently broke limits and barriers and gained influence over many. The power of Christ Jesus defied the law of physics and broke through traditional religious ideas and practices. In fact, what set Jesus apart was the power he carried wherever he went. The crowds who followed Jesus always marvelled at the power he displayed, whether it was healing the sick or raising the dead. Jesus manifested the power of God on Earth. Jesus' power had no limits, boundaries, or impossibilities.

Because it comes from God, the power of Jesus Christ is limitless. It has no boundary or cap. "I am the Alpha and the Omega, the First and the Last, the Beginning and the End" (Revelation 22:13).

As his followers, we have only to ask in his name to claim our part in his redemptive powers and salvation. "Very truly I tell you, my Father will give you whatever you ask in my name" (John 16:23).

How Did Jesus Use His Powers?

Jesus was a man of power, a man who defied natural laws, which surpassed the understanding and the abilities of other men. As Jesus preached to his followers, he operated in signs, miracles, and wonders. This power could only be manifested by his authority from God.

During his time on Earth, Jesus demonstrated his miraculous powers in many ways. John tells us that he performed many more miracles than those captured in the gospels (John 20:30). Here are some of the miracles the gospels described:

> He walked on water and defied the natural laws. (Matthew 14:22–34)
>
> He turned gallons of water into wine for guests at a wedding. (John 2:1–11)
>
> He fed five thousand people with only five loaves of bread and two fish. (Matthew 14:13–21)

He healed the sick, lame, blind, and those possessed by demons. (Matthew 15:30)

Many people who were once dead, such as Lazarus, were restored to life by Jesus. (John 11:1–44)

He commanded nature by calming a furious storm. (Mark 4:35–41)

He caused the miraculous catching of fish where there were none previously. (Luke 5:1–11)

He had a supernatural ability to know what others were thinking or know their history, such as the Samaritan woman by the well. (John 4:1–42)

- Demons bowed before Jesus Christ in the fullness of his authority because even they understood that he was Lord. (Mark 1:23–24)

Although Jesus was a man of great power, he understood that his power was to be exercised under the authority of his Heavenly Father for the benefit and purpose of God's kingdom.

In all his supernatural ability—there was a balance of power and humility. Power and humility were bonded together in the life and ministry of Christ as he lived on the Earth.

Not only does Jesus have power, but he offers his power freely to those who chose to follow him. Through building and establishing a relationship with Jesus Christ, we also have access to his power. We have the ability to become partakers of his kingdom and his authority. Therefore, if we have a relationship with Jesus Christ, we are not limited in power because he lives inside of us. There is nothing that we cannot fulfill.

PRAYER

Lord Jesus, may we know your power, may we see your power, and may we act in your power. In Jesus' name, amen.

CHAPTER 13

JESUS UNLIMITED

Man directs us to Christ, but the Holy Spirit connects us to him.

Jesus and the Holy Spirit

I am confident that as you have come this far in this book, you have gained a greater understanding of who Jesus is, his place in the Holy Trinity, and the importance of following him. It is my prayer that as you read this chapter, you will be enlightened with a whole new perspective of who Jesus is. I believe this chapter will expand your view and revelation of the knowledge of Christ.

Previously in this book, you came to the knowledge of the Holy Trinity. You may be wondering about the relationship between Jesus Christ and the Holy Spirit. I want you to know that Jesus is within the Holy Spirit, and the Holy Spirit is within Jesus. They are both divinely intertwined. You might say that the Holy Spirit is *Jesus unlimited.*

As you will recall, Jesus was conceived and brought forth by the grace of the Holy Spirit (Matthew 1:20–23). Jesus was born out of the spirit. In the womb of his mother Mary, he was formed and brought forth from the supernatural to become a natural being. Without the creative power of the Holy Spirit, Jesus would have never been conceived and brought forth on Earth.

You will also recall that after Jesus' baptism, the Holy Spirit descended upon Jesus, and a voice from heaven proclaimed, "You are my Son, whom I love; with you I am well pleased" (Mark 1:9–11).

So, not only did the Holy Spirit form and bring Jesus forth, but he also communicated God's message to Jesus on Earth.

The Holy Spirit also acts as a supporting agent for the work of Jesus' ministry. Before his death, Jesus spoke to his disciples, preparing them for his departure from Earth. Jesus encouraged the disciples by telling them that though he may be absent physically, God will send an advocate in Jesus' name, called the Holy Spirit, to remain with them and assist in the kingdom work (John 14:16–26).

The Holy Spirit as Connector

Although Jesus is no longer physically available on the Earth to humanity, his spirit through the Holy Spirit is available to us all. We are neither orphans nor lost sheep; we are equipped and empowered by the Holy Spirit. The Holy Spirit acts as a connector to Jesus. The Holy Spirit is our advocate.

The Holy Spirit's job is to remind us of the ways of Christ and everything he taught, to bring us into his revelation, and to empower us to follow him. The Holy Spirit serves as everything that solidifies our relationship with Jesus. Based on the Book of Isaiah, early church fathers ascribe seven virtues to the Holy Spirit: wisdom, understanding, counsel, fortitude, knowledge, piety, and fear (awe) of the Lord.[9]

Jesus Christ worked in unity with the Holy Spirit while on Earth. We initially see the unity of Jesus and the Holy Spirit manifested during his conception in his mother's womb (Luke 1:35). Then again, we see the Holy Spirit manifested as a dove out of heaven during the day of Jesus' baptism (John 1:32). This is one of the key reasons it is important that we understand the Holy Spirit.

For us to truly dive deeper in our journey with Christ, we must understand the correlation between Jesus and the Holy Spirit. Jesus promised his disciples that when he physically leaves the Earth, the Holy Spirit sent by God would replace Jesus' physical presence (John 14:26). The Holy Spirit is assigned to continue the work of Jesus Christ and must be given our attention and love.

The Holy Spirit is one of the greatest linking agents to Jesus Christ. Truly, without the Holy Spirit, we cannot be one in unity with Jesus. The Holy Spirit enables us to intimately know Jesus, understand his ways, hear his voice, and walk in his power. We must not forget that when we walk in unity with the Holy Spirit, we are also walking in unity with Jesus.

When we connect and lean on the Holy Spirit, he enables us to cling to Jesus. The Holy Spirit will make sure we are connected to Jesus so that we remain in him and follow the path he set for us.

PRAYER

Holy Spirit, I know you are my very source of connection to Jesus. Guide me, Holy Spirit, so that I may know him. In Jesus' name, amen.

CHAPTER 14

REPENTANCE

Repentance does not simply mean we will no longer do the unwanted action. It means we are turning over our lives to the one who is worth more.

What Does Repentance Mean?

When you look at a typical dictionary definition of *repent*, it means to "feel or express sincere regret or remorse about one's wrongdoing or sin."[10]

However, the biblical definition for repentance comes from the Greek word *metanoia*, which means a change of one's mind or a "transformative change of heart."[11]

Repentance is more about transforming our hearts than it is to be staying away from a specific sin or temptation. Jesus desired most that those who would encounter him would be transformed. It is his desire that we would become new people, fully regenerated by the power of his spirit. How then can we be transformed without repentance?

Change of Heart and Mind

Finding Jesus not only requires us to follow his teachings, study his lifestyle, and practice the attributes of his character, but it also encourages us to have a change of mind and a change of life. No one who truly encounters Jesus Christ ever remains the same as they were before.

Many examples in the Bible show that repenting means renewing the mind and understanding. For example, the Samaritan woman at the well in John 4 did not know Jesus or what he was teaching, nor was she seeking an encounter with him. But when she had an encounter, it was a life-changing one. The Samaritan woman repented not only because she regretted her sins and wrongdoings but because she had a change of heart and mind.

The reason Jesus gave his life for you and me as a precious sacrifice is because he desires for us to have a change of heart and mind. The cost of our sins is his sacrifice, and we make repentance by following him and changing our lives.

Repentance begins with having a change of heart, change of mind, and change of life. Jesus gives us the ability to repent as we follow him because we begin a new life in him.

What Does Repentance Assure Us?

Repentance assures us that our relationship with Jesus Christ is real and true.

Repentance assures the outside world that we are truly in a relationship with Jesus, and we are no longer the same. Many people think repentance means that we will never again fall short of the glory of God, but this is untrue. In fact, the disciples fell short over and over again, but this did not alter the state of their repentance. Their hearts remained transformed, and their overall lives showed evidence of this supernatural transformation. Think about the woman at the well or Mary Magdalene. If they had not turned away from their old selves and transformed, many would say they did not truly encounter Jesus. Even the disciples had to be transformed before following the lead of Christ.

Our willingness to repent displays the level of intimacy we desire to have with Jesus. Throughout scripture, this is not something Jesus makes optional. Jesus wants to shine through your life; he wants people to see him through you. When you decide to repent through his power, people will begin to gravitate to the one who was able to transform you.

Remember that repentance is never a natural decision, nor can it be performed in your own strength. Repentance takes an open heart and an open spirit to receive the grace of the Father. We cannot repent in our own wisdom or ability. It is all made possible through Jesus.

In essence, repentance is not simply regretting the mistakes you have made. Instead, repentance is realizing that a change needs to be made in your life and that change is available through following Jesus Christ.

PRAYER

Lord Jesus, today I confess and repent. I confess that I am a sinner. I need your grace and forgiveness. Wash me and make me whole that I may come into a new life with you. In Jesus' name, amen.

CHAPTER 15

WORDS OF JESUS

Jesus changed the world. There is no doubt of that. His life is so significant that we still read his words, teachings, and wisdom two thousand years later. Many of his words are echoes of the teachings he learned from the Jewish scriptures in the Old Testament. Many other sayings are unique to his life and teachings.

Often when quoting Jesus, we tend to gravitate toward the familiar stories and words of Christ. This chapter contains some of his less well-known quotes, along with explanations of what his words mean. Reading his words helps enhance our understanding of his teachings and strengthen our relationship with him.

What Jesus said	What it means
"If anyone comes to me and does not hate father and mother, wife and children, brothers and sisters—yes, even their own life—such a person cannot be my disciple" (Luke 14:26).	We understand here that Jesus is telling us that following him may cause a certain level of strife and contention in our lives, but it is the cost of following him.

What Jesus said	What it means
"While Jesus was still talking to the crowd, his mother and brothers stood outside, wanting to speak to him. Someone told him, 'Your mother and brothers are standing outside, wanting to speak to you.' He replied to him, 'Who is my mother, and who are my brothers?' Pointing to his disciples, he said, 'Here are my mother and my brothers. For whoever does the will of my Father in heaven is my brother and sister and mother'" (Matthew 12:46–50).	Jesus wants us to understand that when we truly follow him, we are automatically adopted into his family. We now become his brothers, sisters, sons, and daughters. Jesus is offering us an opportunity to be a part of his loving family and to have a great depth of intimacy with him.
"If the world hates you, keep in mind that it hated me first" (John 15:18).	Jesus knew that he was never truly liked by the Jewish authorities. This is evident in his interactions with Pharisees, Sadducees, and Jewish leaders. They did not like what he stood for and who he was. Likewise, as a follower of Jesus, you may come across people who don't necessarily like you. This has nothing to do with you, but rather it is connected to whom you stand for.

What Jesus said	What it means
"Anyone who hates a brother or sister is a murderer, and you know that no murderer has eternal life residing in him" (1 John 3:15).	In the days of Jesus, sin was rampant. People displayed hate, jealousy, and envy. Jesus wants us to understand that we must love our neighbour as ourselves. Our neighbour is our brother or sister since we are all formed by the hands of our creator. When we display hate, we kill, we destroy. This is not the path to eternal life.
"But anyone who hates a brother or sister is in the darkness and walks around in the darkness. They do not know where they are going, because the darkness has blinded them" (1 John 2:11).	We cannot hate and walk in the light. In order to walk in the light of Jesus, we must love. Love = Light. Hate = Darkness.
"Everyone will hate you because of me, but the one who stands firm to the end will be saved" (Mark 13:13).	Although you may be disliked because of your stance for Jesus, you have an assurance that if you stand firm, you will gain eternity with him.
"Love your enemies and pray for those who persecute you, that you may be children of your Father in heaven. He causes his sun to rise on the evil and the good, and sends rain on the righteous and the unrighteous" (Matthew 5:44–45).	Jesus loved his enemies, and so we are called to do as well. Our enemies are also God's creation, and as such, we must love and pray for them.

What Jesus said	What it means
"My kingdom is not of this world. If it were, my servants would fight to prevent my arrest by the Jewish leaders. But now my kingdom from another place" (John 18:36).	Jesus understood that though he had all power and authority in the Earth, his kingdom and rulership were not in the Earth's domain. Jesus understood that his true kingdom was in heaven.

JESUS' MINISTRY IN ISRAEL

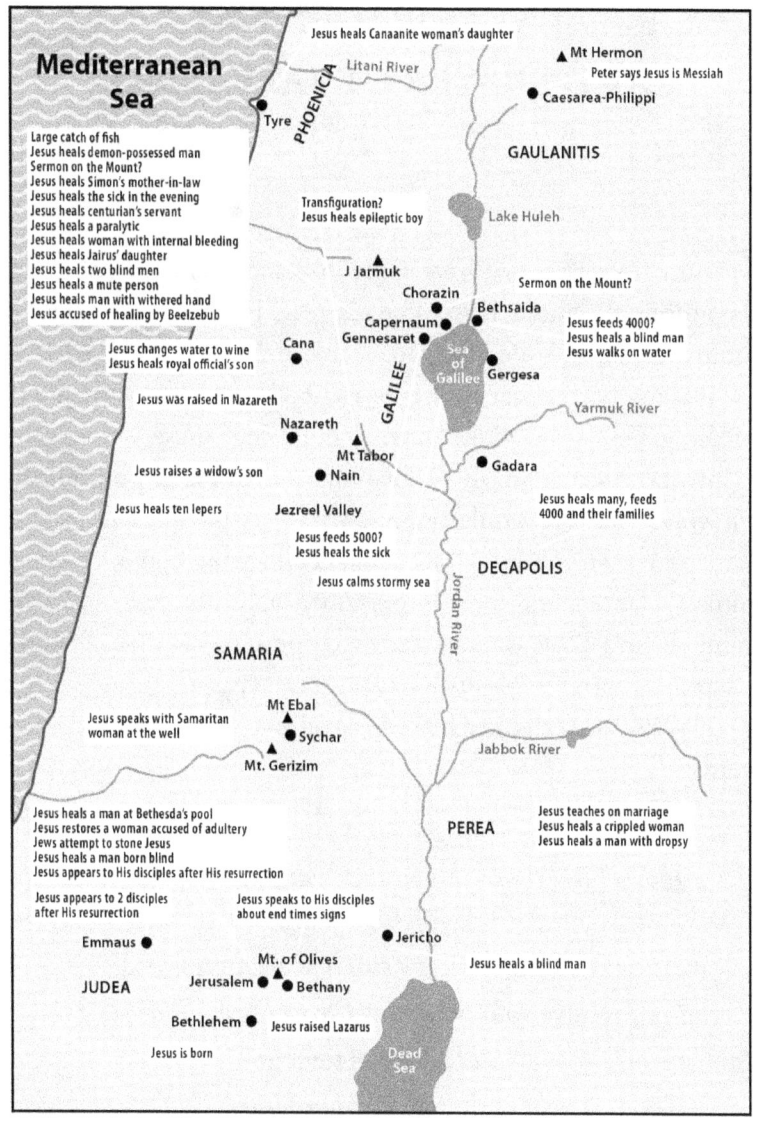

ENCOURAGEMENT AND PRAYER OF SALVATION

It is my hope that you have come into a greater depth of understanding of Jesus Christ. Jesus is real. He lived, he came, he conquered, and he died for you.

It is my prayer that your eyes and heart would be enlightened by the grace of the Holy Spirit. I hope that these writings and scriptures will not simply be chapters and words to you but that the words you read would become your very pursuit and reality.

I pray that you give Jesus a chance in your home, marriage, ministry, family, and most importantly, your life. Jesus loves you so much, and all he wants is an invitation into your life. Will you accept him into your heart today?

If your answer is *yes*, I would love that you could pray these words:

Heavenly Father, I am a sinner.
Today I ask that you wash me with the blood of your
Son Jesus Christ.
Forgive me of all my sins and transgressions.
Today, I receive your Son Jesus Christ (Yeshua) as my Lord
and personal saviour.
I believe that he was born, died, and

was resurrected on the third day.
I receive him in my heart.
May I be transformed and renewed by his spirit.
In Jesus' name, amen.

If you prayed this prayer, I would like to take this opportunity to welcome you to the family of faith as a sincere believing Christian. You are truly not alone, as there are billions of people across the globe in this same family in spirit. I encourage you to connect with a Bible-believing group of Christians and grow in your journey with Jesus Christ.

Peace and blessings,
Frank Boahene

ABOUT THE AUTHOR

Frank Boahene is devoted to faith in Jesus Christ and to spreading the message of hope and life of the gospel. Frank presently serves within the body of Christ in Ontario, Canada. Frank is a lover of Jesus, lover of people, and lover of life. He is a father to his lovely children, husband to his beautiful wife, Mary Boahene, and leader and mentor to many in ministry. His time is mostly spent with his loving family and in mentoring, training, and raising up leaders for the church. Frank Boahene also preaches, teaches, and evangelizes to souls within and outside the church.

Frank is also an honorary graduate with a Bachelor of Religious Education from Tyndale University. He continues to pursue education further so that he can reach those who are seeking purpose and teach them that Jesus is available.

Through years of ministry, devotion, teaching, preaching, mentoring, and discipling, Frank has connected with and encouraged many souls to follow and believe in the gospel of Jesus Christ. This is his continued goal, mission, and purpose in life.

END NOTES

Chapter 4
1. https://en.wikipedia.org/wiki/Genealogy_of_Jesus
2. https://en.wikipedia.org/wiki/Significance_of_numbers_in_Judaism
3. https://en.wikipedia.org/wiki/Genealogy_of_Jesus

Chapter 5
4. https://en.wikipedia.org/wiki/Life_of_Jesus_in_the_New_Testament
5. John 18–19; Matthew 26–27; Mark 14–15; Luke 22–23
6. https://en.wikipedia.org/wiki/Crucifixion_of_Jesus
7. https://en.wikipedia.org/wiki/Resurrection_of_Jesus

Chapter 7
8. https://www.britannica.com/topic/agape

Chapter 13
9. https://en.wikipedia.org/wiki/Seven_gifts_of_the_Holy_Spirit

Chapter 14
10. https://www.lexico.com/en/definition/repent
11. https://www.merriam-webster.com/dictionary/metanoia

With every donation, a voice will be given to the creativity that lies within the hearts of our children living with diverse challenges.

By making this difference, children that may not have been given the opportunity to have their Heart Heard will have the freedom to create beautiful works of art and musical creations.

Donate by visiting
HeartstobeHeard.com

We thank you.

www.ingramcontent.com/pod-product-compliance
Lightning Source LLC
Chambersburg PA
CBHW070629050426
42450CB00011B/3149